NIC BISHOP
SPIDERS

Written and photographed by
Nic Bishop

SCHOLASTIC INC.

Spiders are meat eaters, like lions and tigers.

But they are much more scary!

Crab spiders hide on flowers.

Jumping spiders lurk among leaves.

Their spider senses know when *prey* is near.

Hairs on a spider's body can feel vibrations and movements. Spiders can taste with their feet.

And when a spider senses food,
it pounces!

A spider injects its prey with venom using its fangs. Then the spider oozes *digestive juices* on its meal. This turns the prey's insides to goo, so the spider can suck them into its stomach.

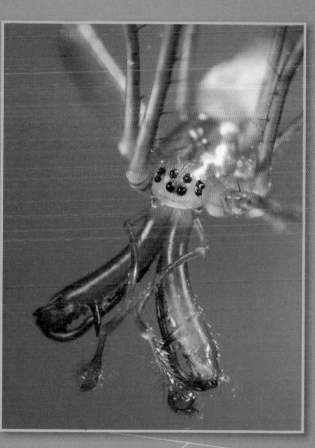

A spider's stomach is in
the front part of its body.
This part is called the
cephalothorax. It is where
the spider's eight legs and
eight eyes are, too.

The back part of a spider's body is called the *abdomen*. It has the spider's heart and the *spinnerets*, which make silk.

Spider silk can be stronger than steel and super stretchy.

Tarantulas spin silk sheets in their dens. Jumping spiders spin silk safety lines as they move around. These help them find their way home again.

Garden spiders spin sticky
silk webs.

When an insect gets trapped,
the spider wraps it in more silk.
Then the spider eats it.

As a spider grows, it sheds its hard skin. This is called *molting*.

The new skin is soft and stretchy. Then it dries and turns hard, like a suit of armor.

When a male spider has grown up,
he looks for a female.

A jumping spider does a special
dance for the female, so she
recognizes him. Otherwise she
might mistake him for a meal.
She might eat him!

A female spider wraps her eggs in a soft, silk case.

Some spiders look after their egg cases. Other spiders hide them away.

Baby spiders look like little adults.

They spin silk. They have fangs and spider senses. They are ready to find prey.

A Closer Look with Nic Bishop

I have traveled all over the world looking for spiders. I have also raised several at home. I watched over them for months as they grew up so that I could photograph rare events like molting and laying eggs.

Spiders make interesting houseguests. One big spider learned to push open the lid of its cage and tried to build a new home behind my bookcase. Another ended up on the ceiling. I even had to take a few spiders that needed special care on vacation with me. Luckily for me, my wife likes spiders, too!

Glossary

abdomen: the back part of a spider's body, where its heart and spinnerets are

cephalothorax: the front part of a spider's body, where its stomach, legs, and eyes are

digestive juices: what a spider uses to break down food in order to eat it

molting: shedding an outer layer of skin

prey: an animal that is hunted by another animal for food

spinnerets: the part of a spider that makes silk

Photo Index

jumping spider,
front cover

baboon tarantula,
page 1

wolf spider,
pages 2–3

crab spider,
pages 4–5

bold jumping spider,
pages 6–7, 8–9

rose-hair tarantula,
page 10

long-jawed spider,
page 11

fishing spider,
pages 12–13

black widow spider,
pages 14–15

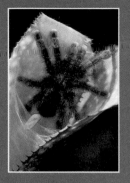

pinktoe tarantula,
pages 16, 26–27

golden brown jumping
spider, page 17

black-and-yellow garden
spider, pages 18, 19

cobalt-blue tarantula,
pages 20, 32

Thiodina jumping spider,
pages 22–23

Selenocosmia tarantula,
page 24

Goliath birdeater tarantula,
page 29

huntsman spider,
back cover

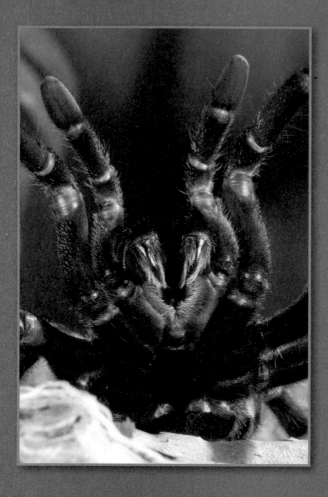

ISBN 978-0-545-23757-4

Copyright © 2012 by Nic Bishop

12 11 10 9 8 7 6 5 4 3 2 1   12 13 14 15 16 17/0

Printed in the U.S.A.   40

First printing, September 2012